LANDS OF BELONGING

For Milun and Mani. For the story you are part of, and the stories to come.
D. and V. Amey Bhatt

For Ammi, Thaththi, Kumudu, Surani, Susantha, and Kalum.
S. Perera

First published 2022 by Nosy Crow Ltd
Wheat Wharf, 27a Shad Thames
London, SE1 2XZ, UK

Nosy Crow Eireann Ltd
44 Orchard Grove, Kenmare,
Co Kerry, V93 FY22, Ireland

www.nosycrow.com

This edition published 2025

ISBN 978 1 80513 748 1

Nosy Crow and associated logos are trademarks
and/or registered trademarks of Nosy Crow Ltd.

Text © Donna and Vikesh Amey Bhatt 2022, 2025
Illustrations © Salini Perera 2022, 2025

Consultancy provided by Dr Rajbir Hazelwood, historian of South Asia and Modern Britain.
Sensitivity reading provided by Javerya Iqbal and Rachel Faturoti.

The right of Donna and Vikesh Amey Bhatt to be identified as the authors and
Salini Perera to be identified as the illustrator of this work has been asserted.

All rights reserved.

This book is sold subject to the condition that it shall not, by way of trade or otherwise,
be lent, hired out or otherwise circulated in any form of binding or cover other than that in
which it is published. No part of this publication may be reproduced, stored in a retrieval system,
or transmitted in any form or by any means (electronic, mechanical, photocopying, recording
or otherwise) without the prior written permission of Nosy Crow Ltd.

The publisher and copyright holders prohibit the use of
either text or illustrations to develop any generative machine learning
artificial intelligence (AI) models or related technologies.

A CIP catalogue record for this book is available from the British Library.

Printed in Italy following rigorous ethical sourcing standards.

Papers used by Nosy Crow are made from wood
grown in sustainable forests.

1 3 5 7 9 8 6 4 2

LANDS OF BELONGING

A History of India, Pakistan, Bangladesh and Britain

Donna and Vikesh Amey Bhatt · Salini Perera

Contents

Welcome!	6
What Makes You, *You*?	8
Inventive Ancient India	10
One Land, Many Religions	12
Ancient Indian Empires	14
The Dazzling Delights of India	16
One Land, Many Kings	18
Building an Empire	20
The World at War	22
Dividing a Country	24
Independence for India	26
From South Asia to Britain	28
A Place to Call Home	30
Racism and Uprisings	32
South Asian Culture Today	34
Bold South Asian Flavour	36
Party Time!	38
Fireworks, Food and Fasting	40
A Day in Your Life	42
South Asian Customs	44
Do You Speak South Asian?	46
Fun and Games!	48
Amazing South Asians	50
Amazing South Asians Today	52
A South Asian Calendar of Celebrations	54
Time to Reflect	56
What Happened When?	58
What Happened Next?	60
Glossary	63
Index	64

Welcome!

You might think things that are Indian, Pakistani or Bangladeshi are easy to spot, such as brightly coloured temples, tall-towered mosques or supermarket shelves stocked with ingredients to make hot, spicy curries. But other things may surprise you, from words you use every day like 'pyjamas', to yoga classes or even washing your hair with shampoo.

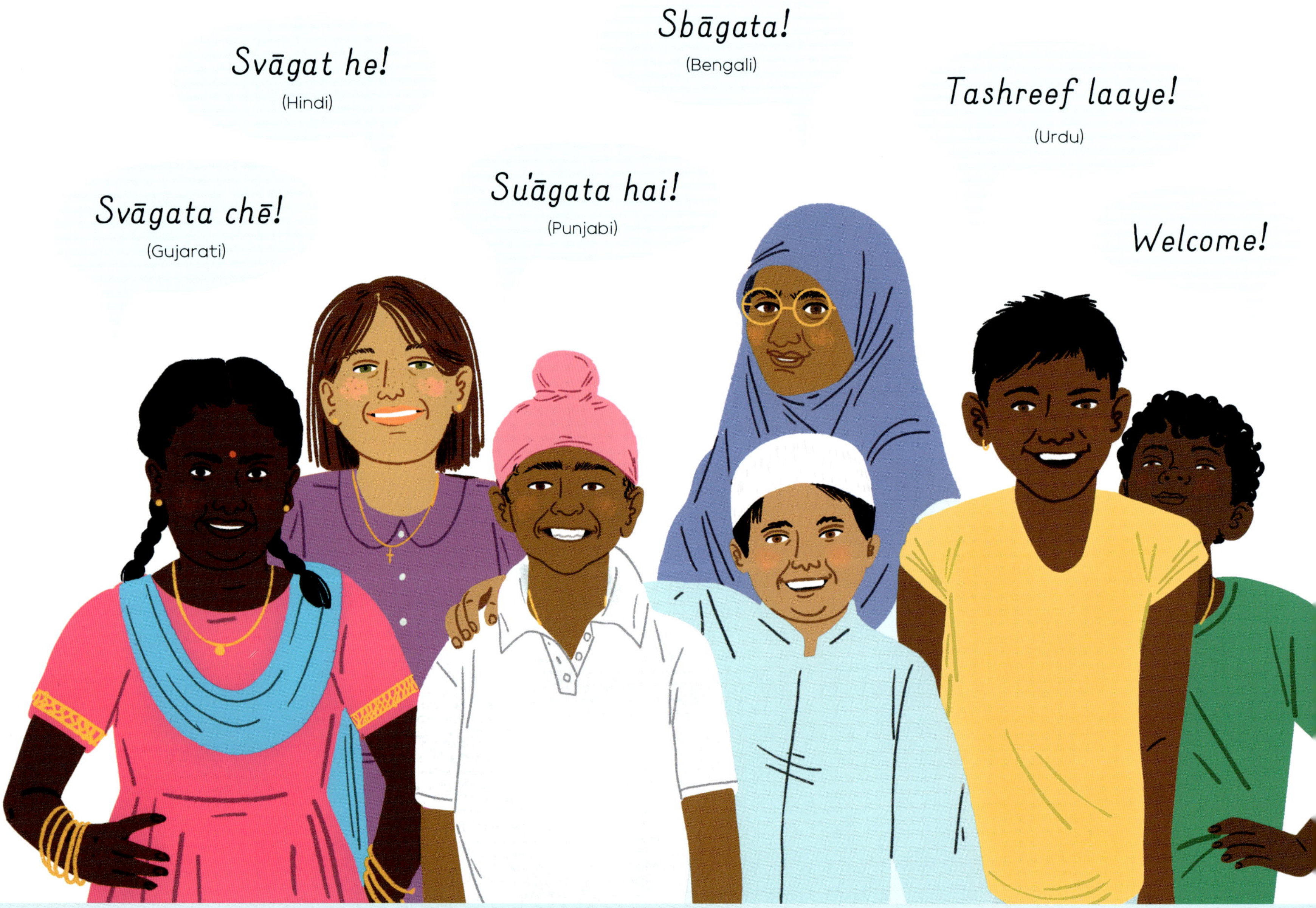

Svāgat he!
(Hindi)

Sbāgata!
(Bengali)

Tashreef laaye!
(Urdu)

Svāgata chē!
(Gujarati)

Su'āgata hai!
(Punjabi)

Welcome!

REARRANGING SPACES

The invisible lines that separate one country from another are called borders, and they can change over time, usually because rulers disagree about what land belongs to which country. The name of a country can change too, depending on who is in charge. Bangladesh and Pakistan are quite new countries – less than a hundred years ago they were both part of India.

The History Mystery

The United Kingdom has a huge number of people living in it whose family stories began in India, Pakistan or Bangladesh. Often, the story of how South Asian and British history is tightly linked together isn't explained in schools or in books.

The way that we learn about our past is decided by the people who record our history. There are many different ways of telling the same story, and what you write down and how you write it depends on your point of view, such as if you think some events and people are more important than others.

For hundreds of years, the wealthy in Britain were educated enough to read and write, so we know a lot about what they thought of themselves and of the world. But being taught to read and write was much less common for people who lived in South Asia, so written historical stories from a South Asian point of view are much harder to find.

This book aims to piece together how South Asian and British history are connected. You might find it interesting, surprising and sometimes very sad – but for the people of South Asia, and for South Asians in Britain, the future is full of hope and excitement.

Turn the page to discover why Indian, Pakistani and Bangladeshi history *is* British history.

WHERE IN THE WORLD?

India, Bangladesh and Pakistan, along with Bhutan, Nepal, Sri Lanka, Afghanistan and the Maldives, are all in the southern part of Asia, one of the world's seven continents. People from these countries are sometimes called 'South Asians'.

GREAT OR UNITED?

The United Kingdom (UK) as we know it today is made up of England, Scotland, Wales and Northern Ireland. Great Britain is made up of England, Wales and Scotland. The United Kingdom is tiny compared to the size of India, Pakistan and Bangladesh.

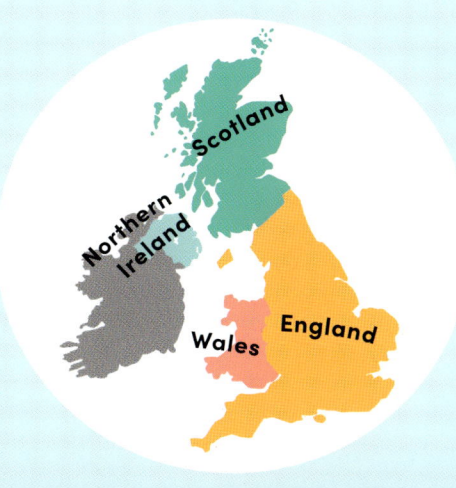

What Makes You, You?

When asked to describe yourself, it can be hard to know where to begin. You might start by saying something about the way you look, such as having curly hair or freckles. Perhaps you could mention the things you enjoy or are really good at, or even something you really hate, like going to bed when it's still light outside!

All the things that make you, *you*, form different parts of your identity.

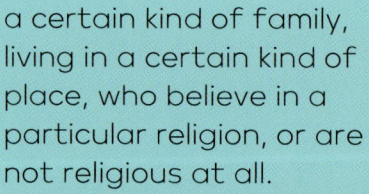

Some people might feel that their identity is simply something they were born into:

a certain kind of family, living in a certain kind of place, who believe in a particular religion, or are not religious at all.

Others might say that what makes you, *you*, are the experiences you've had throughout your life.

Often, no matter what you think of yourself, other people might describe you differently. They might focus on only one aspect of your personality, looks or history, when in fact all of us are many things.

Where Are You Really From?

How important is where you were born, where your parents were born and where your grandparents were born, to who you are today? Having a sense of who you are and where you're from isn't as simple as having the place you were born written in your passport. For people whose family trees begin many miles away, it can be complicated.

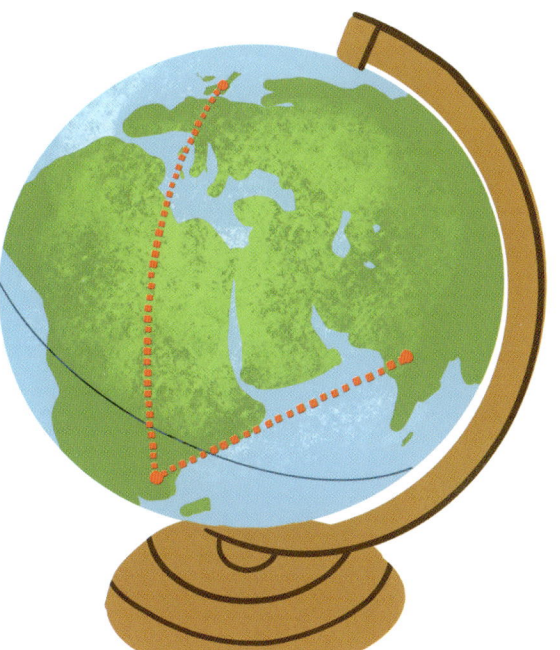

Take Vikesh (who's written this book), for example . . . He was born in Ealing, in London, in England, to parents who had arrived in the United Kingdom from Tanzania in East Africa four years before, whose own parents fled Gujarat in India after their home became unsafe to live in.

Vikesh has never lived anywhere but the United Kingdom, but he understands his parents' language which is a mixture of Gujarati and Swahili (the language of Tanzania). He grew up following Hinduism, one of the main religions in India, and if you saw him, you would probably say that he 'looks Indian'.

He loves fish and chips with curry sauce, puts chilli on his eggs in the morning, and sometimes says 'panjama', the Swahili word for pyjamas.

He counts in his head in English, replies in English when he is spoken to in Gujarati, and remembers cheering on Great Britain, when the Olympic Games were in London, as one of the best days of his life.

When people ask Vikesh, 'Where are you from?' what should he say? London? The United Kingdom? Africa? India? Asia?

Inventive Ancient India

Ancient India was a land of inventors, big thinkers and skilled tradespeople. Archaeologists (people who study history by examining objects) have found evidence of ideas and inventions being used in ancient India that were far more advanced than anything in Europe at the time.

Fine Craftsmanship

The first people to grow cotton for making cloth were the Harappan people, also known as the Indus Valley Civilization, in the area of modern-day Pakistan around 4,500 years ago. Over thousands of years, expert clothmakers perfected their weaving techniques and dyed their cotton in vivid colours, using ingredients such as pomegranate seeds and turmeric, which grew in India's warm climate.

INDIA THEN AND NOW
When we talk about India *before* 1947 in this book, we are talking about the lands of India, Pakistan and Bangladesh. Before this date they were all one country.

It wasn't until after the invasion of India by Alexander the Great of Greece in 327 BCE – over 2,000 years later – that trade in cotton began with the ancient Greeks and Romans. By this time, Indian cotton was so incredibly fine it was often mistaken for silk.

Ancient Indian people also developed special ways of working with iron which were not used in Europe until around 1,500 years later. The seven-metre-tall iron pillar of Delhi has been standing since around 400 CE.

As Easy as One-Two-Three

Around 1,500 years ago, Indian mathematicians developed the Hindu-Arabic numeral system, a way of writing numbers that was much simpler than the Roman numerals commonly used at the time. Roman numerals are letters that represent numbers, so 1 = I, 5 = V and 10 = X, and so on. Depending on the order of the letters, you add or subtract numbers to reach your total figure, and that's before you even do any sums! The Hindu-Arabic numeral system is also known as the decimal system, and is made up of the numbers 0, 1, 2, 3, 4, 5, 6, 7, 8 and 9. This clever way of writing numbers didn't catch on in Europe until about 500 years later!

Not long after the invention of the decimal system, another impressive mathematical development came when an Indian astronomer named Brahmagupta defined zero as the result of subtracting a number from itself, and proposed rules for calculating negative numbers. (You could say, he invented nothing!)

The ancient Indian approach to healthcare, known as *Ayurvedic* medicine, is to care for the body and soul together, based on the belief that the two are very closely connected. It was practised in India around 1000 BCE, hundreds of years before Hippocrates, the ancient Greek 'father of medicine' was born!

There is also evidence of advanced surgery in ancient India, with records from as far back as around 600 BCE instructing surgeons on how to reconstruct a person's nose if it had been cut off – the procedure is still known as the 'Indian Flap' today.

This surgery was important because cutting off a person's nose was a common punishment in ancient India. The idea was that everyone who saw a person with no nose would instantly know they were untrustworthy. Having a nose rebuilt by surgeons could once again allow a person (rightly or wrongly accused of crime) to live a more normal life.

CHECKMATE!

Chess as we know it today was invented in India around the 6th century. It is thought to have evolved from an older Indian game called *Chaturanga*, which may have had four players instead of just two – and used elephants instead of bishops!

One Land, Many Religions

In ancient India, many religions and belief systems flourished side by side. Buddhism, Hinduism, Jainism and Sikhism all began here. Islam was introduced in around the 7th century, and Christianity is believed to have arrived between the 1st and 3rd centuries. Although many other religions are also practised in modern-day India, Pakistan and Bangladesh, these six remain the most followed.

Buddhism

People who follow Buddhism are known as Buddhists. Instead of believing in any gods, most Buddhists respect and worship the Buddha who was the founder of their religion, a man named Siddhartha Gautama. Buddhists believe in *karma*, which means that everything you do, both good and bad, will have a consequence. The *Tripitaka* is their most important book.

Hinduism

Hindus are people who follow Hinduism, which is the oldest known religion. Hindus believe in a main god called Brahman who takes on many forms called deities. Hindus often have statues of the deities in their homes to worship. They believe that once you die, you will be reborn into a new life depending on how you spent the one you are currently living – this is known as reincarnation. They follow a collection of sacred texts called the *Vedas*.

Jainism

Jains are followers of Jainism. They do not believe in any gods but do believe in perfect people who have lived their lives well and who are worthy of worship. They believe in both karma and reincarnation, and strongly believe in looking after the planet and all living beings on it. They follow holy texts called the *Agamas*.

Sikhism

A person who follows Sikhism is called a Sikh. Sikhs believe there is only one God, which they call Waheguru. They also believe that all people are born equal and that all living beings, including animals, have a soul. Sikhism was founded by Guru Nanak, the first of the ten Sikh Gurus – these were people believed to live pure lives and who set a good example for others. Sikhs also believe in karma and reincarnation. Their holy book is called the *Guru Granth Sahib*.

Islam

Muslims are followers of Islam. Muslims believe in one true God called Allah, and follow the teachings of Allah's messenger, Prophet Muhammad. To live a good life, Muslims believe in the Five Pillars of Islam, which are declaring your faith, praying five times a day, giving money to charity, fasting during the holy month of Ramadan and performing a special pilgrimage to the religious site of Mecca in Saudi Arabia at least once. The *Qur'an* is the Islamic holy book.

TYPES OF FAITH
Religious texts are long, complicated and are understood in different ways by different people. Because of this, almost every religion is followed by groups who understand their main religious texts differently and practise in alternative ways.

Christianity

A person who follows Christianity is called a Christian. They believe in one God who is revealed in three forms, as the Father, the Son and the Holy Spirit. Christians believe that Jesus Christ, God's son, was sent to live as a human, to teach people to love his father and their own neighbours. Christians also believe Jesus died to save humans from their sins and was brought back to life by God. Their holy book is called the *Bible*.

THE POWER OF BELIEF
Even today, four of the six most followed religions in the world have Indian origins. After Christianity, Islam has the largest number of followers across the world.

Ancient Indian Empires

Unlike many modern countries, ancient India wasn't ruled by just one group or family. There wasn't one government, emperor or queen making laws for everyone. Instead, ancient India was often split into regions which were governed by different rulers or royal families. This meant that the language, religion and rules of one part of the country could be completely different to the next.

There were also many disagreements as to which rulers owned and governed what land, with frequent wars taking place to decide who ruled where.

When we speak about groups of places that are ruled by a specific family, government or person, we sometimes refer to them as 'empires'. These places don't need to be next to each other, or even have much in common. Usually when an empire takes control of a new region or country, it does so by force and the people who live in the conquered land have no choice but to go along with the new leader's laws and rules.

A Few of Ancient India's Most Powerful Empires

Around 320–185 BCE

Mauryan Empire

Starting in the east of India, the Mauryan Empire was the very first empire to cover almost all of India, and some parts of Iran too. A senior minister within the empire named Chanakya is thought to have written one of the earliest known books about how to run a country, and believed the key to success was to have a large network of spies.

Around 30–375 CE

A Kushan statue of the Buddha from around 100–200 CE.

Kushan Empire

Ruling over much of the countries now known as Tajikistan, Uzbekistan, Afghanistan, Pakistan and northern India, the Kushan Empire spread the Buddhist religion across previously mostly Hindu lands, and became rich by developing links between the Silk Roads from the Far East and the ports of the Arabian Sea.

Around 320–550 CE

Gupta Empire

Beginning in the northeast, the Hindu Gupta Empire ruled over most of northeast, northwest and central India for centuries. This period is sometimes known as the 'Golden Age of India' due to the many inventions and discoveries that took place during this time.

The numbers 0–9, also known as the decimal system, were invented during the Gupta Empire.

1526–1858

Mughal Empire

The Muslim Mughal ruling family were experts in agriculture and trade and were incredibly rich. They were also the first rulers to try and create a united India where Hindus, Muslims and people of other faiths lived side by side. This tolerance lasted for roughly the first 200 years or so of their rule.

Built by Mughal emperor Shah Jahān, the Taj Mahal is one of the world's most famous buildings.

Maratha Empire

The Marathas were a Hindu warrior group who came from the southwest of India. Starting with just one small territory and 2,000 men, they fought the mighty Mughals and went on to rule over much of central and northern India. They built over 300 hilltop forts as part of their defences, many of which you can still see across India today.

1674–1818

1206–1556

Delhi Sultanate

India's first Islamic kingdom was ruled over by a series of sultans from the area that is known as Delhi today, giving the empire its name. Over hundreds of years, the sultans built many cities and great mosques, including the *Qutb Minar*, one of the tallest minarets (a tower used to call Muslims to prayer) in Asia.

1799–1849

Sikh Empire

Founded in what would now be Pakistan, this empire of Sikh warriors ruled over a small part of China as well as parts of Afghanistan, Tibet and India. Established by Sikh warrior Ranjit Singh, one-time owner of the world-famous *Koh-i-Noor* diamond, his empire fell apart within ten years of his death in 1839.

INDIAN ROYAL NAMES

We often hear of Indian leaders being called different names, but what do they mean?

- **Maharaja:** a king
- **Maharani:** a queen, or wife of a king
- **Rajah:** a prince
- **Rani:** a princess
- **Emperor:** a male who rules over an empire
- **Empress:** a female who rules over an empire

The Dazzling Delights of India

Over 400 years ago, during the reign of the British Queen Elizabeth I, the thought of India, a country famous for its spices, silk and jewels, was dazzling.

At first, whenever British merchants wanted to buy luxury goods from India, they had to purchase them from other nearby countries such as Portugal or the Netherlands, which had already set up special businesses to trade with India. This was expensive and meant the British traders had to sell the goods on for an even higher price in Britain, so only the very richest people could afford them.

The British soon realised that to be able to have all the spices and cotton they liked, they would need to travel to India themselves.

In 1600, Queen Elizabeth I gave permission for 218 British merchants to form a business called the East India Company. They were to sail across the Indian Ocean to the East Indies (which we would call the islands of southeast Asia today) to trade with the islands and with India.

With Britain being an island, it was already equipped with lots of ships and people who knew how to sail them in all kinds of conditions, and their experience, knowledge and skill paid off. Trading with India made a lot of money for many of the Indian people who lived there, as well as for the British traders who came to buy from them.

A Fighting Business

For the first 150 years or so of its existence, the East India Company acted like a messenger between the rulers of India and the government and ruling kings and queens of England, carrying lavish gifts which were exchanged between the British and Indian royalty. However, from 1757, other countries started trying much harder to trade with India. To drive out the competition, the East India Company began bringing an army along with its ships.

Trade and Slavery

On the surface, the East India Company looked to be a business making things that were hard to get hold of in Britain, such as new fabrics and spices, available to many more people.

But over the many hundreds of years the company existed, it also played a role in slavery. Between the 1730s and the 1770s, its huge fleet of ships were regularly used to transport enslaved people from their homes in Africa (and other places such as Indonesia) to different countries where they would be forced to work without payment for their whole lives and were treated very badly. This trade in enslaved people and the goods they produced made countries such as Portugal, France and Great Britain very wealthy.

One Land, Many Kings

When the English East India Company was formed in 1600, India didn't have just one ruler. Instead, it was split up into kingdoms governed by different kings and maharajas, who often disagreed about which parts of the land they ruled over.

Sometimes, the East India Company would lend carefully chosen Indian leaders its army, to help fight on their behalf. This made the East India Company a lot of money. It also meant that the people in charge could find out important information about how different Indian kingdoms were being run, in order to look for opportunities to gain more power.

After violently winning a number of important battles, the Treaty of Allahabad was signed in 1765 between Lord Robert Clive of the British East India Company and Mughal emperor Shah Ālam II. This law gave the East India Company the right to rule over and collect taxes from the people of Bengal, a huge area of land (which we would call West Bengal and Bangladesh today), Bihar and Orissa (now known as Odisha).

The East India Company would never have been able to take charge of the whole of India all at once. But because there were so many small kingdoms with armies far weaker than its own, it gradually took power, kingdom by kingdom, until it ruled over the entire land.

Buying Power

It can be hard to imagine a company ruling a country. Like most businesses, the aim of the East India Company was to make as much money as possible, not to look after a huge country full of people, making sure children went to school and that anyone unwell could find a hospital.

To make things even more difficult, the people who ran the East India Company came from Britain and knew very little about what living in India was like, or what was important to the people who called it their home.

As a result, the people of India had laws forced on them that went against their religious beliefs. They were paid badly for their work and were expected to do jobs they didn't want to do. They also had to pay very high taxes. If they couldn't pay, they would be punished, or even killed, meaning many families went hungry, as they had to sell all the food they grew to pay their bills instead of feeding themselves.

Despite living in fear, the people of India tried to fight back. Over 100 years later and after many unsuccessful attempts, the Indian War of Independence in 1857 finally forced the British government, and Queen Victoria, to step in.

INDIANS OF THE ROYAL COURT

Although Queen Victoria never travelled to India herself, she did have Indian people in her court. Princess Gouramma of Coorg was one of them. Her father had given her to the British in exchange for protection for his kingdom. One of Queen Victoria's many godchildren, Princess Gouramma grew up in the royal palaces and died when she was 23.

Building an Empire

By the time of the Indian War of Independence, the government of Great Britain had already been using its army to take over other countries for hundreds of years. This process was called 'colonialism'.

COLONIALISM

The word 'colonialism' is used to describe one group or country taking control of another. 'Colonists', or settlers, take over land and resources to make themselves richer, while the traditions and needs of the local people are often ignored or repressed.

CANADA
1763–1982, 219 years
Traded in wood, meat and fish and metals such as gold, iron and copper.

NORTH AMERICA
1607–1783, 176 years
Traded in wood and tobacco (a dried leaf which is smoked or chewed).

Because the East India Company was making Britain so much money, ordering it to give power back to the people of India was not a very appealing option. So, in 1858, the British government decided that it would rule over India by force instead, adding the country to its growing empire.

Queen Victoria, Great Britain's reigning monarch, made herself the Empress of India and the country's head of state. This began what is sometimes known as the 'Time of the British Raj'.

A ROYAL NAME

Raj means 'rule', 'king' or 'emperor'.

WEST INDIES
1763–1833, 70 years
Traded in enslaved people, sugar cane, spices and rum.

Britain's Moneymakers

By 1913, Great Britain ruled over almost a quarter of the Earth's land and its people – the largest empire the world has ever seen. As in India, the people that the British ruled over were often treated cruelly and unfairly, with little respect for their religious values, and were forced to work hard to make Britain money. Many people rose up to try and fight for their freedom. But Britain was so powerful that few countries succeeded.

Many other countries from all over the world made a lot of money for Britain while they were part of the empire, from the Republic of Ireland (which was ruled by Britain for over 700 years) to Egypt, Jamaica and Hong Kong.

RULING BY RAIL

The effects of British rule were felt all over the world. In South Asia, the East India Company (and later the British Empire) began building the first long-distance railway line across India in 1853. The railways helped the British to move their armies quickly to put down any uprisings. Trains were also used to transport food for the British to sell, leaving the local people hungry. South Asian people couldn't even use the trains to travel safely: the second- and third-class carriages they were allowed to use were dirty and overcrowded, resulting in illnesses spreading easily.

INDIA
1858–1947, 89 years
Traded in spices, sugar and pigment for dyes and cotton.

BENGAL
(WEST BENGAL IN INDIA AND BANGLADESH)
1757–1947, 190 years
Traded in jute (a plant-based material used for making rope and fabric), wood and cotton.

BRITISH WEST AFRICA
(THE GAMBIA, SIERRA LEONE, GHANA AND NIGERIA)
1821–1888, 67 years
Traded in enslaved people, palm oil and sugar, cocoa beans, wood and gold.

CEYLON
(SRI LANKA)
1815–1948, 133 years
Traded in tea, coffee and cocoa beans.

AUSTRALIA
1788–1901, 113 years
Traded in sheep's wool, dairy produce and metals such as gold and copper.

BRITISH EAST AFRICA
(KENYA, UGANDA, ZANZIBAR AND TANZANIA)
1895–1963, 68 years
Traded in coffee, cotton and tobacco.

SOUTH AFRICA
1806–1961, 155 years
Traded in precious materials such as gold and diamonds, as well as meat, fruit and feathers.

NEW ZEALAND
1851–1907, 66 years
Traded in sheep's wool, dairy produce and metals such as gold and copper.

FROM EMPIRE TO COMMONWEALTH

Some countries that were once part of the British Empire have chosen to belong to the Commonwealth of Nations, a group of 'free and equal' countries that share a joint history of living under British rule. The British monarch is seen as the head of the group, and the aim of the organisation is to create a bond of friendship and support between nations.

The World at War

At the beginning of the 20th century, two wars involved so many countries they became known as the First and the Second World War. They are often thought of as European wars, because that's where they started, but soldiers from all over the world were involved.

Both wars saw Britain relying on its empire for much more than just making money. Britain had powerful enemies it could not defeat alone. As a result, the British army was made up of soldiers from across the British Empire.

THE FIRST WORLD WAR
- Up to 1.5 million Indian soldiers volunteered
- More than 50,000 died
- Indian soldiers made up almost 17 per cent of the total British army

THE SECOND WORLD WAR
- Over 2.3 million Indian soldiers signed up, the largest volunteer force in history
- Up to 24,000 died
- Indian soldiers made up almost 29 per cent of the total British army

Fighting for Freedom

It might seem strange to go and fight for a country that isn't your own. But Britain was able to offer soldiers from some of the places they controlled a much-wanted prize: independence – the chance for their countries to be free of British rule.

With this in mind, Indian people were told that fighting for Britain would mean freedom for India – if Britain won. So many beloved fathers, sons, brothers and husbands believed that joining the British Indian army and risking their lives was a worthwhile price to pay.

SOLDIERS OF INDIA
At this time, Pakistan and Bangladesh had not yet been created. When we talk about Indian soldiers here, this includes volunteers from the areas of modern-day Pakistan and Bangladesh.

One Army, Two Standards

During the First World War, Indian soldiers were initially in charge of the dangerous work of transporting supplies to battle sites where movement by rail or road was no longer possible, using horses and mules. Most were not even given weapons. But Indian recruits went on to become key to every part of Britain's defences, from fighting in the trenches during the First World War to flying fighter planes in the Royal Air Force in the Second World War.

Despite the constant bravery and hard work of the Indian recruits, high-ranking positions within the army were kept for soldiers from the British Isles. The British army at the time held the incorrect view that Indian soldiers lacked leadership, and that they would not be given the respect needed to lead soldiers in battle.

Indian recruits in both wars were often transported to places that were cold, wet and completely unlike their warm home climates, with soldiers arriving in the middle of winter given very little shelter or means to stay warm and dry. They were paid less than white British soldiers, denied the chance to go home when on leave, and made to live separately to soldiers from the British Isles.

SIKH HEROES
In the Second World War, Sikh soldiers won the highest percentage of Victoria Cross medals out of any British troops.

REMEMBERED FOR BRAVERY

KHUDADAD KHAN was the first Indian soldier to be awarded the Victoria Cross, the highest military award for bravery in the face of the enemy, at just 26 years old. While working as a machine gunner in the Second World War, he held back a German advance alone after the rest of his unit were killed, giving the British time to bring in reinforcements.

NOOR INAYAT KHAN worked as a Royal Air Force radio operator during the Second World War, passing secret messages from France, where she was stationed, to the British government. In 1943, the German secret police discovered Noor was a spy and arrested her. She refused to give them any information and was kept prisoner for a year before being killed. After her death, her bravery was remembered with two awards, the French Croix de Guerre and the British George Cross.

Dividing a Country

During the First and Second World Wars, the British government spent *a lot* of money, much of it borrowed from America, but also from other countries including India. The billions the British now owed meant they could no longer afford the costs that came with governing India, such as providing hospitals, police and running an army.

At the same time, the people of India had been fighting for freedom from British rule. Many Indians followed the example of Mahatma Gandhi, an Indian lawyer and politician, and took part in peaceful marches and protests, while others used violent behaviour to try and be heard. Finally, having played a huge part in helping Britain win both world wars, India's dream of independence was to become a reality.

United by Independence, Divided by Belief

The three main religions in India at the end of the Second World War were Hinduism, Islam and Sikhism. There were many more Hindus than Muslims, and a lot more Muslims than Sikhs. While most people agreed India should be free of British rule, some thought the country should be divided to allow Muslims to have their own state (their own land and government), so they could live under their own religious laws. The idea of splitting the country was known as 'Partition'.

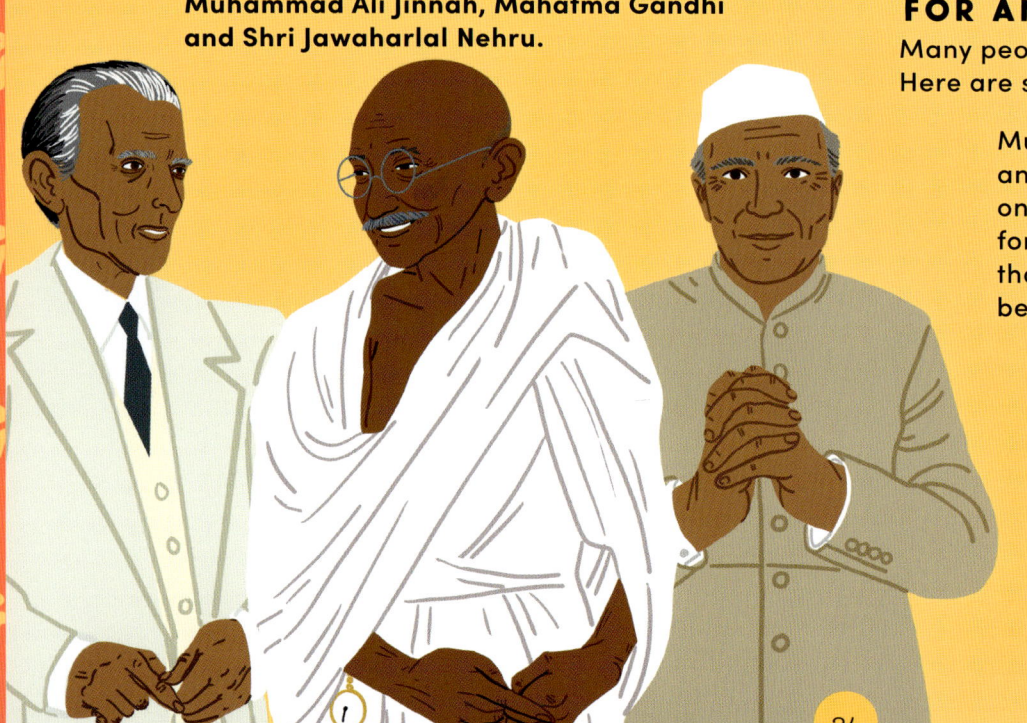

Muhammad Ali Jinnah, Mahatma Gandhi and Shri Jawaharlal Nehru.

FOR AND AGAINST PARTITION

Many people campaigned either for or against partition. Here are some of the most well-known campaigners:

Muhammad Ali Jinnah was a barrister, politician and campaigner for Partition. He believed that one government for all people would work better for Hindus because there were more of them, and that issues were important to other faiths would be overlooked.

Lawyer and leader of the non-violent resistance against British rule, Mahatma Gandhi believed that all Indian people should continue living together.

Shri Jawaharlal Nehru fought passionately for India's independence, resulting in years in prison. Initially against Partition, he went on to support the idea and was elected as India's first ever Prime Minister.

A five-pointed star and crescent moon: the symbol of Islam.

The khanda: one of the symbols of Sikhism.

Om: the symbol of Hinduism.

The Birth of Pakistan

Eventually, the British government decided that as well as becoming independent, India would be divided into two, creating a new Muslim state called Pakistan. While at the time there were a few distinct Hindu and Muslim areas, across most of the country, people of different religions lived side by side. For the British, this meant that deciding how to divide India was very difficult.

DRAWING A LINE

British lawyer Cyril Radcliffe was employed by the British government and given just five weeks to decide the fate of almost 400 million people. Before travelling to India, the furthest Cyril had been was France, and in the rush to make Partition happen quickly, he was given out-of-date maps and inaccurate information about India's population. He had no understanding of where different religious communities lived, or why, and instead divided India using information about railways and rivers.

Independence for India

The people of India were told they would be granted independence by the last day of June in 1948, but in fact the country stopped being part of the British Empire almost a whole year earlier on 15th August 1947. Just 48 hours after India was declared independent, British troops stationed in India to defend the British Empire began sailing home, leaving the country in chaos.

The Wrong Side of the Line

Imagine being told one day that because your religion is different to the religion of your next-door neighbour, one of you has to leave. What would that mean for your street? Where do you think you would go?

Independence had been long-awaited in India, and when it came it was greeted with joy. However, two days later, Britain's decision about how to partition India was announced, and suddenly millions of people found themselves living in the 'wrong' country.

The newly created West and East Pakistan were to become the homelands of the Muslim population, while India was to be home to Hindus, Sikhs and those of other faiths.

Because of Britain's new borders and the new religious divide, families in Pakistan and India suddenly found themselves homeless, even if they had lived in the same place for centuries. People had to pack up their belongings and leave, without any idea of where they should go. Families, including the elderly and crawling babies, travelled for miles – mostly on foot – in search of a new home, with barely any food or clean water.

Refugee Specials

Some trains had been arranged for people moving from one country to the other called 'refugee specials'. But as Partition led to the largest ever number of people moving all at once, there were not nearly enough of them. Passengers were crammed into carriages and even travelled on train rooftops, with no way to keep clean or use the toilet. On arrival, refugees were often met by criminals who looted the few belongings they had left, and many were sadly killed while travelling.

When refugees from both countries finally did arrive at their new homes, they were often very angry, and sometimes if they discovered people living in the 'wrong' place they would violently force them to leave. Muslim, Sikh and Hindu monuments were also torn down if they were on the 'wrong' side of the Partition line.

Divided Forever

The violence that followed Partition continued for many years, and sensitivities between India and Pakistan still exist today. After Partition, instead of migrating to India or Pakistan, many people chose to move to countries in Africa, or other countries that had a connection to the former British Empire.

In 1971, everything changed for a second time. When Partition was announced, West Pakistan and East Pakistan were on completely different sides of India, and the people of each area lived very differently. After years of disagreements, East Pakistan declared itself independent of West Pakistan, becoming its own country: Bangladesh.

THE HUMAN COST OF PARTITION
- Around 15 million people moved to a new home within just four years
- Up to 2 million people are thought to have been killed in the violence that followed
- 400,000 refugees walked in a single line from Pakistan to India

From South Asia to Britain

We have evidence of people from the Indian subcontinent (now known as India, Pakistan and Bangladesh) living and dying in Britain since the middle of the 16th century, before the famous English playwright William Shakespeare was even born, and decades before British merchants began regularly sailing to India to explore and find new things to bring home.

That said, these records are few and far between, probably because most of the information we have about people living in Britain over the past 500 years or more, comes from Christian churches. Records came from things like baptisms (when a person officially commits to following Christianity), weddings and funerals, and as most South Asian people were not Christian, there are few records of their presence or important life events. Because of this, it is very possible there were more South Asian people in Britain over the past 500 years than we will ever know.

A Perilous Journey

Early trips between South Asia and Britain would have been long, uncomfortable and extremely dangerous because of the changeable weather conditions over such vast oceans. The risk of being shipwrecked was a constant threat, with about five per cent of the East India Company's ships being wrecked or lost at sea.

Other dangers included being attacked or imprisoned by pirates or killed by infectious diseases. Even scurvy – a disease virtually unheard of today caused by a lack of vitamin C from fresh fruits and vegetables – could kill sailors on the six-month voyage between continents, and on arrival, travellers would encounter yet more new illnesses and infections which their bodies might not be able to fight off.

The high risk of such journeys meant that a person would only make the trip from South Asia to Britain if they believed there to be something really brilliant at the end of it – or if the choice wasn't their own. The long journey also meant that nobody intended to visit for just a few weeks. They would either be planning to start a new life in Britain or stay for a number of months at the very least – before making the equally treacherous journey in the opposite direction.

Who Were the First South Asians in Britain?

LASCARS

South Asian sailors, known as lascars, were cheaper to employ than British seamen, and often worked as chefs, deckhands and stokers (engine-room workers). Their British employers believed they were better able to stand the fierce heat of a ship's engine rooms because of the warm climate of their homelands.

AYAHS

These nannies were employed by rich European families in South Asia, and then bought back to Britain. Sometimes they were employed to look after children for the journey only, and not given a job once they arrived. A ticket home was incredibly expensive, so many ayahs found themselves stranded.

SERVANTS

South Asian servants were thought to bring distinction to a household, and often featured in British family portraits as a way to show off their wealth. Queen Victoria was known to have had South Asian servants and members of her court.

MERCHANTS

Some South Asian businesspeople knew they could make more money selling their goods in Britain than they could in their homelands, so ambitious merchants packed up as much stock as they could before travelling across the ocean to make their fortune.

ARTISANS

South Asian crafts used materials and methods never before seen in Europe. This meant that people who were skilled in making certain things could make a lot of money if they made the long journey and set up businesses in Britain.

TAKEN BY FORCE

Not all South Asian people made the journey willingly or for work. Some were wrongfully taken from their homes and sold to wealthy families, such as a teenage boy known as 'Julian', who was taken from Madras (now known as Chennai) in 1720 and 'gifted' to a Mrs Elizabeth Turner. She used him as entertainment and made him dance for her guests. Desperately attempting to escape the situation, Julian took money to start a new life, and set the house he had been held captive in on fire. He was sentenced to death.

A Place to Call Home

Walking around parts of Britain today, you will see many wonderful and different South Asian people and communities. Often, you might notice colourful sari shops, places of worship, and traditional South Asian food shops and restaurants, all in the same few streets.

Although South Asian people have lived and worked in Britain for centuries, to begin with most settled not far away from where they arrived by ship. As time went on, many found partners and moved to find homes all over the country, while others lived with the rich families they worked for, either on country estates or in big cities.

A Call for Help

It wasn't until around 1947 that South Asian people started coming to Britain in very large numbers, especially from India, West Pakistan and East Pakistan (now known as Bangladesh). After two world wars, much of Britain was in ruin, and citizens from all over the Commonwealth were encouraged to move to the UK by the British government to help rebuild the country. At the same time, many Indian and Pakistani people were fleeing violence caused in their home countries by the Partition of India.

There was a particular shortage of people who could work in hospitals, textile mills, airports and transport systems, so the British government encouraged new arrivals to move to parts of the country which were in desperate need of skilled workers. That is why many South Asian communities are concentrated in particular areas.

Building the NHS

South Asian doctors were also recruited for the new British National Health Service. These early pioneers arrived with as little as £3 in their pockets (about two day's wages or £100 by today's standards) due to strict rules on how much money they could carry. Can you imagine starting an entirely new life in a totally different country with no money to spare or savings?

In return for rebuilding Britain, subjects of Commonwealth countries could become British citizens automatically until the early 1960s, when the British government began passing a series of laws, called the Commonwealth Immigration Act, making it harder and harder for people from the Commonwealth to make Britain their home.

South Asian Hotspots

These are just some of the places that South Asian migrants settled, and where you'll still find amazing South Asian buildings and communities today:

1. SCUNTHORPE
Famous for its steelworks, which were in desperate need of skilled workers after the Second World War.

2. LEICESTER
Belgrave Road, also known as 'the Golden Mile', gets its impressive name as it was once believed to be home to the most shops in Britain selling gold outside of India. Now it's full of authentic curry restaurants and places to buy traditional South Asian clothes. It also hosts what is widely thought to be the largest Diwali celebrations outside of India.

3. EALING (LONDON)
The first Sri Lankan Buddhist temple in Britain and the first Buddhist monastery outside of Asia, the London Buddhist Vihara was founded in 1926. Now located in Chiswick, it is still home to *bhukkus* (Buddhist monks) today.

3. SOUTHALL (LONDON)
Close to Heathrow airport, as well as a rubber factory, both of which urgently needed skilled workers after the Second World War.

3. NEASDEN (LONDON)
You'll find an impressive Hindu *mandir* (temple) here. The BAPS Shri Swaminarayan Mandir is carved entirely from stone. Over 8,000 tonnes of it, in fact, which was shaped by 650 artisans in a small town called Kandla in India. Around 23,000 individual pieces were then shipped to the United Kingdom and assembled like a giant jigsaw puzzle by over 1,000 volunteers!

4. WOKING
Britain's first permanent purpose-built mosque opened here in 1889. Queen Victoria's Indian servants and her advisor, Abdul Karim, worshipped here whenever the queen was staying at Windsor Castle.

5. CARDIFF
This city was often the first stop for South Asian lascars arriving after a long journey working in a ship's engine rooms.

6. BIRMINGHAM
The city's famous Edgbaston Cricket Ground has often hosted cricket matches between India and Pakistan.

7. MANCHESTER
Manchester University has attracted middle and upper-class South Asian students, particularly from the Punjab region of Pakistan, for at least a century. Since the 1930s many South Asian-run cafés have also existed in the area, bringing overseas students a taste of home.

8. LANCASHIRE
Full of textile factories who needed skilled workers to operate machinery and to produce fabric and clothing.

9. GLASGOW AND EDINBURGH
Glasgow is home to the largest Sikh community in Scotland. The first Sikh Scottish tartan (a material with a particular colour and pattern that represents a Scottish clan) was designed and registered by Edinburgh-based greengrocer Jimmy Singh in 2000.

Racism and Uprisings

Not everyone in Britain welcomed South Asian people, and until the very recent past, laws around treating people equally were not the same as they are now. South Asian people arriving in Britain in the 1950s and beyond, along with other people of colour from all over the world, were frequently turned away from jobs and places to live because of the colour of their skin, their accents and the clothes that they wore.

Signs in hotel and shop windows were regularly seen to say: 'No dogs, No blacks, No Irish' – and by 'No blacks' they usually meant no people who were not white – while some groups of white British people formed organisations to threaten and try to scare off people who came from other countries.

Out of Bounds

Although segregation (the separation of a group of one people from another due to race, class or ethnicity) was never legally recognised in Britain, a version of it existed in plain sight of the authorities until as recently as 1966. This was known at the 'Colour Bar' and meant that in towns and cities across the country, there were places that South Asians and other people of colour were not allowed to work, or even to visit, without fear of violence. What would you say to someone if they refused to let you go somewhere or do something, simply because of the way you looked or the language you spoke?

Rebels or Revolutionaries?

Many new South Asian communities were founded within well-established white British communities. Some white British people felt so threatened by the arrival of their new neighbours that they formed an organisation called the National Front, made up of people who believed that Britain should be for white British people only.

> The National Front was responsible for several racist murders, called for the removal of black and brown people from Britain and protested at airports when new immigrants arrived.

Made-up stories published in newspapers blaming immigrants for a shortage of jobs and housing, and for bringing diseases into towns, helped to spread negative feelings about immigrants across the country.

We often hear about 'rebellions' and 'riots' when we talk about people speaking out about racism – especially if there is a lot of anger involved. In 1979, after many years of violence and the killings of South Asian people and their supporters, a group fighting against racism took to the streets of Southall in London and stood up to the police and the National Front. Violence broke out and one protester, Blair Peach, was killed. No one was ever brought to justice for his death. Is it right to call people 'rioters' and 'rebels' for speaking out against suffering, or do we need to look at the way we examine history and the words we use to describe the past?

A Brighter Future

Today, racism still exists within the United Kingdom. People of colour are more likely to live below the poverty line, be excluded from school, or be arrested by the police among many other examples. Racism can be obvious – people using unkind names or being violent towards others. But it can also be very hard to spot. Lots of small barriers can add up to make people from minority groups feel excluded from things they should be perfectly entitled to, like proper healthcare, support from the government or equal access to jobs.

Social media and the internet can sometimes give people the confidence to say hurtful and harmful things that they would never normally say out loud. But social media and the internet have also given campaigners against racism a powerful tool to stand up against hate. Only by accepting that racism is still a problem can the people of Britain start to work towards becoming a non-racist country.

SPECIAL BROADCASTS

The British government knew that many South Asians coming to Britain in the 1950s would know very little about their new country. So the BBC made special programmes to introduce new immigrants to common British customs, social situations and things such as money and banking. But these were recorded in English rather than in any of the common languages of India, West Pakistan or East Pakistan (Bangladesh), meaning that for many South Asians, a deeper understanding of their new homeland remained out of reach. How easy would you find learning about a new culture in a totally different language to the one you are able to speak?

South Asian Culture Today

People from South Asia have migrated all over the world to start new lives for centuries, and since the 1950s many have chosen to make Britain their home. Despite the challenges of moving from one country to another, over the years many South Asian families and communities have flourished across the United Kingdom.

The impact of South Asian culture can be felt in every part of our lives, from our health practices to the clothes we wear, the music we listen to and the food we eat.

Mind, Body and Spirit

Today, yoga is a popular activity around the world, but it's only relatively recently that it has been practised outside of South Asia. No one can say for certain exactly when it was invented, although many claim its roots come from the Indus Valley Civilization in the area of modern-day Pakistan around 5,000 years ago. One of the main aims of yoga, which is both a philosophy (a way of thinking about the world) and a physical practice (sometimes called *asana*), is to create harmony between the mind, body and spirit.

Today, many people who live busy lives use yoga as a way to unwind and look after themselves. Traditionally, yoga was sometimes used as a way to pray, but now it is also used in lots of other ways too. Some people see it as a way purely to stretch and exercise, and some people see it as a way to meditate. People can start practising yoga when they are very young, and there is no such thing as being too old for yoga.

Yoga for All

You might think of yoga as being very still and quiet, but there are lots of different types – maybe you could try one of these?

YIN YOGA
Yin is a type of yoga where you try to stay very still, and hold poses (movements) for a long time. It allows the joints of the body to relax more deeply into stretches, and makes you feel very calm.

VINYASA YOGA
This is a form of yoga where you don't stop moving, with one pose linking to the next in a dance-like way. It is good for improving both strength and flexibility. Classes can be fast-paced, very energetic and make you sweat!

YOGA NIDRA
The perfect yoga to do before bedtime, Nidra is a guided meditation that allows you to focus on your body after a busy day. The aim is to find relaxation in a place between wakefulness and sleep.

SPECIAL INGREDIENTS

Scented and special oils are very important to many South Asian people. Rooted in thousands of years of tradition and ritual, oils play an important part in day-to-day life, whether it's for religious reasons, health benefits or a well-needed weekly pamper.

For many South Asians, a weekly hair massage with coconut oil is an important ritual for healthy and strong hair, while homes are cleansed and kept pure by burning *diya* lamps filled with a special kind of scented oil. South Asian babies also often receive oil massages, as massage and baby development are believed to be closely linked. Known as *maalish*, baby massage not only has health benefits but is a sign of affection and love.

We also see oil massages during South Asian wedding rituals. Oil and turmeric are made into a paste to give the bride and groom a full body rub. Afterwards their skin not only feels great but looks radiant and ready for the big day!

Bold South Asian Flavour

The influence of South Asian food is found everywhere, all over the world. From the spices we use every day – such as black pepper, grown on the Malabar Coast of India, to the cinnamon from Kerala that we sprinkle on our doughnuts – it's hard to imagine how we'd add flavour to our dishes without South Asian ingredients.

A Little Bit Spicy!

Chilli is one of the most important spices in South Asian cooking, but you might be surprised to learn that the Indian, Bangladeshi and Pakistani food eaten in the United Kingdom today is often quite different to what might be considered traditional.

When South Asian chefs first began cooking in Britain, they were introduced to new ingredients and equipment they hadn't used before. The result was that dishes such as the 'balti' (invented in Birmingham) and the 'tikka masala' were born. These milder, sweeter and creamier dishes felt exotic to British customers, while being closer in flavour to the foods they were used to eating.

A Taste of Home

Many Indian restaurants in Britain today are run by people originally from Bangladesh, whose families came to the United Kingdom in the 1960s to escape the violence that followed Partition. While some saw opportunities to start a new business in the catering trade, others wanted to give their friends and families a place to be together and have a taste of home.

Curries from different regions can have completely different flavours and ingredients. Take these for example . . .

BANGLADESHI CURRY
Bangladeshi food often uses seafood and fresh fish, as the country has a large coastline and many rivers. Poppy seeds, mustard seeds and mustard oil are common ingredients too.

INDIAN CURRY
Most northern Indian curries are water-based, although in southern India coconut milk is often used instead. The dishes are thick, spicy and can be vegetarian or meat-based.

PAKISTANI CURRY
Mutton (lamb) and beef are common ingredients in Pakistani curries. Pakistani food also includes barbecued food too, such as grilled meat and kebabs.

South Asian Table Manners

No matter what you eat, there's one important way to eat it. Using your right hand (never your left), scoop the food on to a flatbread, naan, roti or chapati with a twist of your wrist. Use your fingertips to bring the food to your mouth. It's important not to bring the plate to your mouth, lower your head instead. It's best to take small amounts of food each time, and make sure the food doesn't touch your palms. Don't put your fingers in your mouth – use your thumb to push the food inside. Easy!

The Taste Test

There is a delicious Indian, Pakistani and Bangladeshi dish for every occasion!

FOR A COLD WINTER'S DAY, try *daal chawal* (a thick, spicy type of lentil stew) and boiled rice with a *kachumber* (tomato salsa) and mint chutney.

FOR AN EVERYDAY DISH, try *khichdi*, a mix of rice and daal (lentil stew) with lots of butter and a choice of different pickles.

FOR A FAMILY GET TOGETHER, try *seekh kebab* (skewers of minced meat mixed with spices and herbs) grilled on a barbecue, with *pav bhaji* (potato patties served in a soft bread roll) and *idli sambar* (rice cakes with a coriander sauce and lentil stew or daal).

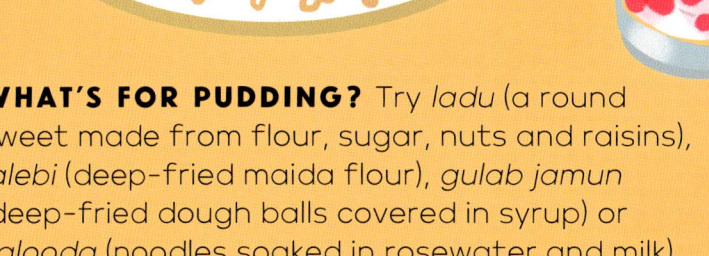

IF YOU LIKE IT SPICY, try chilli chicken, *masala dosa* (a rice flour pancake often filled with spiced potato) and *masala* fish (fish fried in very hot spices).

WHAT'S FOR PUDDING? Try *ladu* (a round sweet made from flour, sugar, nuts and raisins), *jalebi* (deep-fried maida flour), *gulab jamun* (deep-fried dough balls covered in syrup) or *falooda* (noodles soaked in rosewater and milk).

Party Time!

Something many South Asians have in common is that they love to party! Some South Asian dances have specific moves that need to be learned, but others are easy for anyone to join in.

Garba

From the Indian state of Gujarat, this dance involves groups of people (often all women, but sometimes men too) who form circles, one within another. All the dancers in one circle move round in the same direction, while dancers in the next circle move in the opposite direction. If you don't know the moves, don't worry – there will be a nearby auntie who can show you what to do.

Dancers may also be given sticks which are used to click together with other dancers – these are called *dandiya*. People might dance a *garba* in community spaces, or before a wedding.

WHAT TO WEAR?
Women often wear *chaniya cholis*, colourful skirts and blouses that are hand-embroidered with mirrors and shells. Men may wear *kurtas*, long, loose, collarless shirts, with tighter trousers called *churidars*.

MANY AUNTIES
Your family aren't always the people you're related to by blood, they can be close friends too! Many South Asian people refer to friends of their families as aunties, uncles and cousins.

THE SOUND OF MUSIC

How many of these instruments do you recognise?

A *tabla* can be played on its own, or as an accompaniment to singers.

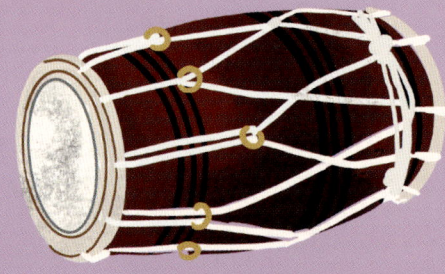

Dholak drums are great for bhangra!

You only need to use one hand to get a great sound from these finger-sized cymbals known in Bengal as *kartals*!

Bhangra

Bhangra is a type of folk dance originating from the Punjab region of Pakistan and India, and it is *loud*! It is danced to the sound of large *dhol* drums being hit with cane sticks, which creates a deep bass beat.

It's performed at Sikh, Hindu and Muslim weddings and other big celebrations, and the dancing style uses lots of big arm and shoulder movements. Sometimes performers use sticks, swords and even sit on each other's shoulders!

WHAT TO WEAR?
Women often wear a scarf called a *dupatta* and a shirt called a *kameez* over some loose-fitting trousers known as *salwar*. Men usually wear kurtas over a large piece of cloth worn around the waist called a *chaadra*. The most important part of a man's outfit is the *pagri* which is worn on the head and needs to be specially tied for every occasion.

Bollywood Dancing

The word 'Bollywood' is used to describe traditional Indian films that are full of energetic music and dancing. Bollywood dancing is influenced by styles from all over the world, not just India, Pakistan and Bangladesh. Traditionally, Bollywood films featured regional folk dances, but today you're just as likely to see R&B and hip-hop-influenced moves. There aren't any strict rules, which is why so many people love it!

WHAT TO WEAR?
Women usually wear either a *sari* or an ankle-length skirt with a short blouse and lots of jewellery. Men usually wear a pleated *dhoti* (a large piece of cloth worn around the waist and tied to look like loose trousers) and often no top at all.

The *sitar* has up to 20 strings, compared to the six strings of a guitar.

QAWWALI

This special way of performing Sufi Muslim poetry is meant to make the singers and listeners feel closer to God. Recently, these energetic musical performances have become increasingly popular outside of India and Pakistan.

Fireworks, Food and Fasting

Did you know that the months of the year aren't the same for everyone? People from some countries and religions often follow completely different calendars and celebrate a huge variety of festivals. There's so much to discover! Here are just a few of the most popular South Asian festivals.

If you want to wish someone well at Diwali, a simple 'Happy Diwali' will do the trick.

Diwali

Known to many as the 'Festival of Light', Diwali is celebrated by Hindus, Jains and Sikhs. The five-day festival usually falls between October and November, and the start date changes yearly as it is worked out using a calendar based on the cycles of the moon.

People from different religions celebrate Diwali for different reasons in different ways. Many people light *diyas* (small clay oil lamps) and homes are decorated with *rangolis* (colourful traditional patterns created on the floor) both inside and out.

For Hindus, Diwali is a celebration of good over evil, while for Jains, Diwali marks an important religious anniversary as well as the start of the New Year. For Sikhs, this is a time to remember *Bandi Chhor Divas* or 'Liberation of Prisoners Day' and think about the importance of freedom and human rights. Celebrations often feature fireworks, special lanterns, music, dancing and plays which tell different religious stories.

Eid al-Fitr

This event in the Islamic calendar marks the end of Ramadan, which is a month of prayer and fasting during daylight hours. *Eid* means feast, and people celebrate with lots and lots of wonderful food! It takes place during the tenth month of the Islamic lunar calendar, on or near a new moon, which means it can fall during different months in different years.

Many people celebrating Eid start the day with prayers in a community space, then go to someone's house for a traditional breakfast. It's also common to visit the graves of lost relatives. People might meet more friends and family in the afternoon and evening – enjoying lots of delicious food along the way. It's a chance to dress up in something special and to be generous to people you love, or those in need, with your time, home and spirit. People often give gifts too, especially to children!

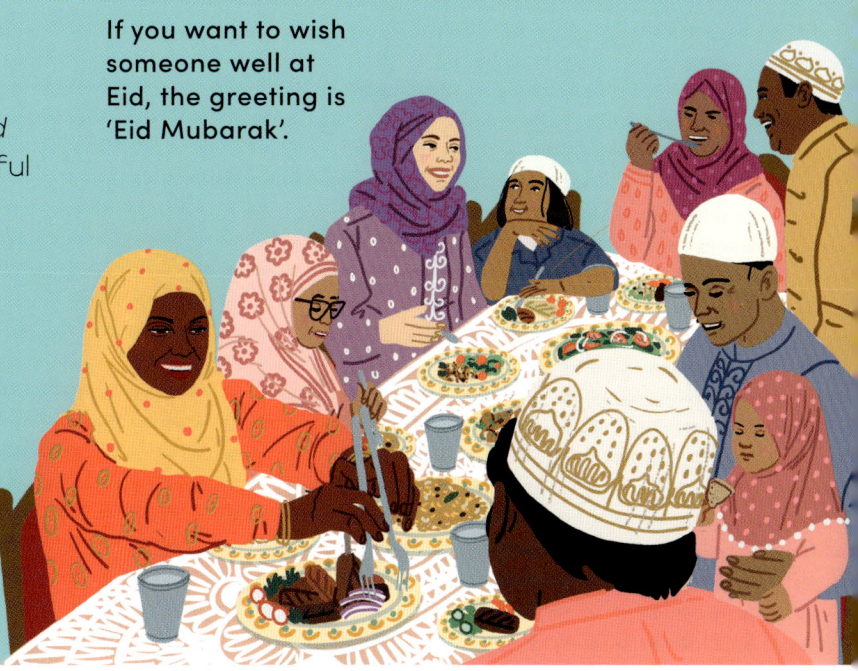

If you want to wish someone well at Eid, the greeting is 'Eid Mubarak'.

Wish someone a great day by saying, 'Wishing you a happy Vaisakhi!'

Vaisakhi

This festival celebrates the day in 1699 that the *Khalsa* was formed, which is the name for the group of people who have officially been baptised as Sikhs. It also marks the start of the Punjabi New Year and is celebrated on the 13th or 14th April. During Vaisakhi, Sikhs visit *gurdwaras* – their places of worship, which are beautifully decorated for the occasion. There they pray and sing hymns from the Sikh holy book – the *Guru Granth Sahib*.

After the service, Sikhs follow their holy book through the streets as part of a beautiful and bright procession called the *Nagar Kirtan*. Everyone wears bright and colourful clothes for the occasion, which is followed by a special meal with family and friends.

Vesak

Also known as 'Buddha Day', this festival celebrates the birth and death of Buddhism's founder, the Buddha, and is usually celebrated during April or May, depending on when the full moon falls. It is also a celebration of 'enlightenment', which is when someone is said to understand the truth about life.

To celebrate, many people visit temples to raise the Buddhist flag and sing hymns. Offerings are also made, such as leaving flowers or burning incense, and some people release paper lanterns into the sky. Families and friends also get together to eat delicious vegetarian food and think about all the good things they have in their lives.

'Happy Vesak' is the best way to greet someone on Buddha Day!

A Day in Your Life

Bringing Indian, Bangladeshi and Pakistani culture into your everyday life is easier than you think. In fact, you're probably already doing it!

Morning! Time for a Wash

The word 'shampoo' was introduced to Britain by Sake Dean Mahomed in the 1800s, and comes from the Hindi word *champi*, meaning 'massage'. Originally from the city of Patna in India, Sake Dean Mohamed worked for the British East India Company before moving to Ireland, and then to Britain, where he eventually opened a bathhouse and spa. He wasn't just good at cleaning hair – he gave great massages too, and even gave treatments to British kings George IV and William IV – how relaxing!

Cup of Tea?

When tea was first brought to Britain in the 1660s, it was extremely expensive, as it had to travel across China to India before being brought to Europe. It wasn't until almost 150 years later that tea was found growing wild in Assam in India, and by 1823 it was on sale in London. Indian tea is now the most popular tea in Britain. In many countries, tea is taken black or with a slice of lemon, but in Britain adding milk and sugar is a much more popular combination.

Brrr! It's Cold Out!

Many of the patterns you might recognise on scarves and other clothes come from original Indian designs, such as the tiny, patterned teardrops known as 'paisley'. The name comes from the Scottish town of Paisley, which made more affordable scarves using the design in the 1800s, as the original, and very expensive, Indian patterned shawls were in such high demand.

Button Up!

Ornamental (decorative) buttons are known to have been used in India by the Indus Valley Civilization (in the area of modern-day Pakistan) as early as 2000 BCE. They were made of carved shells and worn to show how well-off or important a person was. Can you imagine getting dressed without buttons?

Feeling Peckish?

Many of Britain's corner shops were opened and run by people from South Asia who came to live in Britain after the Second World War. Most of these people were highly educated and wanted to run their own businesses, rather than work for other people. Many of these shops have served as community hubs for decades providing food and essential items for local people.

Fancy a Game?

The board game 'snakes and ladders' is based on an ancient game from India called *Mokshapat* or *Moksha Patamu* – the original game was based on the idea of 'morality' (the decisions you make to lead a 'good' life). The squares with the ladders on represented good decisions, while the snakes stood for bad ones.

A Shawl for All

Kashmiri shawls (also known as cashmere), made from the hair of long-haired goats, were traditionally worn by men in India. Queen Victoria was also drawn to their beautiful patterns and luxurious fabric, and the fashion caught on in Britain for both men and women. Today, we know this material as cashmere, and it is still far more expensive than many other types of wool.

Time to Turn In

Cotton was one of the first things to be bought and sold by the British East India Company hundreds of years ago, as the quality of Indian cotton was much finer than the fabrics available in Europe at the time. It's perfect for soft bedsheets even today.

Supper Time!

Not only was Sake Dean Mahomed responsible for introducing British people to the word 'shampoo', he also opened Britain's first Indian-owned and run Indian restaurant in London in 1810. The Hindoostane Coffee House served not only Indian food but sold tobacco too.

South Asian Customs

Every family and culture has their own traditions. The way we greet each other, eat together or use a special word to describe the remote control, all have meaning.

Some of the things we do might not feel familiar to other people, but traditions (usually!) make sense when you know a little bit more about them, and one of the best things is that you can always make new ones up! Here are a few traditions you might recognise that are common for some South Asian families.

Touching Feet

Bowing down and touching the foot of someone older than you is an important mark of respect. Many people believe that the act of bowing down is good for the soul, and that the person bowing will in turn be blessed by the owner of the foot that they've touched.

WHEN MIGHT YOU TOUCH AN ELDER'S FEET?
- When greeting them at birthdays and weddings
- Before going on a long journey
- Before starting something new, like a fresh school year
- Before doing something you're nervous about, like an exam
- When visiting their house, or if they visit yours

Removing Shoes

Most Indian, Pakistani and Bangladeshi people will not wear shoes in the house, and they would expect their guests not to either. As well as being a sign of respect, this is also a practical thing. Shoes have lots of dirt on from walking outside, so taking them off as soon as you get home means less hoovering!

Giving Generously

Giving money as a gift is common for South Asian families, but just any old bank note won't do. Some families add an extra pound to the amount they give you, for luck. So instead of giving someone £10 for their birthday, they'd give a £10 note with an extra pound coin! During Eid, some Muslim elders give younger children small gifts of money called *Eidi* as a celebration of this special day.

Hands-Free Cake!

Cake is of course an important part of any birthday, but many South Asian people get a helping hand eating it! After singing 'Happy Birthday', whoever is enjoying their special day will cut the cake first and then feed it to their friends. Once everyone has had some, the birthday girl or boy will be fed by everyone else, yum!

Sitting cross-legged is sometimes referred to as sitting 'Indian style'.

Sitting Cross-Legged

A table and chairs aren't always necessary when sitting on your own, or with family and friends. Sitting on the floor can be great for your back, and many South Asian people do it regularly as part of their prayer or meditation practice.

Covering Your Head

Special head coverings are often worn by people of all religions from India, Pakistan and Bangladesh. Two you might recognise are turbans, usually worn by Sikh men, and *hijabs*, often worn by Muslim women. Hijabs can be made of beautiful, intricate fabrics for special occasions or be something a little plainer for wearing every day or playing sports.

Do You Speak South Asian?

There are 22 languages recognised in the Indian constitution today, and more than 120 languages each spoken in India by at least 10,000 people. In Pakistan there are two official languages, Urdu and English, plus close to 80 other languages on record, and in Bangladesh, while Bengali is spoken by most people, at least 39 other languages exist.

When you hear South Asian languages being spoken, you might think they sound nothing like English or any other European tongue. But actually, almost half of the people living on Earth today speak languages with an Indo-European root, that is to say, languages that developed from the same starting point – most likely the language of a small group of travelling nomads from the area of modern-day Turkey, or the grass plains of Ukraine and Russia.

The South Asian–English Dictionary

You may not think you know any Indian, Pakistani or Bangladeshi words, but you probably use some every day! How many of these words did you know came from South Asian languages?

BANDANA
from the Urdu word *bandhna* meaning 'to tie'.

BLIGHTY
often thought as a traditional British word for their own country, the word actually came from the Hindi-Urdu word for 'foreign'.

BUNGALOW
means 'house in the Bengal style' in Bengali and Urdu.

CHEETAH
from the Hindi word *cītā* meaning 'leopard'.

CHUTNEY
from the Hindi word *chāṭni* meaning 'to lick'.

COT
from the Hindi word *khāṭ* meaning 'small, light bed'.

DUNGAREE
a word to describe labourers in the Dongri area of Mumbai.

JUNGLE
from the Hindi word *jaṇgal* meaning 'forest, dry land or waterless place'.

LOOT
meaning to steal something, comes from the Hindi word *lūṭ*.

MANTRA
from the Sanskrit word *mantra* meaning 'sacred message or text'.

PUNCH (DRINK)
from the Hindi word *pāñć* meaning 'five' as a fruit punch is usually made with five ingredients.

PUNDIT
from the Hindi word *paṇḍit* meaning 'wise or learned man'.

PYJAMAS
from the Hindi word *pajamas* meaning 'leg clothing'.

SHAMPOO
from the Hindi word *chāmpo* meaning 'to squeeze or massage'.

TANK
from the Gujarati word *tānkŭ* meaning 'reservoir of water'.

YOGA
from the Sanskrit word *yug* meaning 'to join or unite'.

Fun and Games!

How many of these sports did you realise have South Asian connections?

Badminton

This 'feathery' game, originally known as *poona*, looks a little like tennis as it involves rackets and a net. Instead of a ball, the object hit over the net is called a shuttlecock. These days they are usually made of rubber and plastic, but traditionally they were made of cork and goose feathers. *Poona* was invented in India in the 1860s by British army officers – and became known as 'Badminton' after being played on an English country estate of the same name in around 1873.

Polo

Polo, a game where players use special sticks to chase a ball while on horseback was invented in Persia (now known as Iran), but became increasingly popular across India thanks to the conquering Muslim emperors of the 1200s who brought the game with them. The British founded their first polo club in 1859 after being introduced to the game on the tea plantations of Assam.

Cricket

This bat-and-ball game involving two teams of 11 people was invented in the east of England yet is now widely known as India's favourite sport. Cricket was introduced to India during the time of the British Empire, with the first match played in 1721. Even today, India and Pakistan's national cricket teams are fiercely competitive towards each other.

HOCKEY: HOW TO INDIAN DRIBBLE

Hockey is such a popular sport in India that players have even invented a special way to run with the ball! The name 'Indian dribble' was coined during the 1956 Olympics, when the rest of the world noticed the Indian hockey team's incredible dribbling skills.

1 Hit the ball with one side of your stick and move forward.

Kabaddi! Kabaddi! Kabaddi!

Kabaddi is extremely popular in South Asia, but many people in the United Kingdom haven't ever played it, or even heard of it! Want to give it a try? You don't need any special equipment, all you need are a few friends to get started . . .

1. Split yourselves up into two teams. Usually each team has 12 members, with seven playing at a time – but your teams could be smaller if you have fewer people. Give each team an equal area of a field, garden or court.

2. A game lasts 40 minutes in total, with a break to grab a drink and talk tactics at half time. Each team takes turns sending one member over to the opposing team's half of the court. This person is called the 'raider'.

3. The raider shouts 'Kabaddi! Kabaddi! Kabaddi!' while trying to touch as many members of the opposite team as possible before making it back to their own half – they get a point for every member of the opposite team they're able to touch. If they lose their breath and stop chanting (they're allowed to take just one breath during their turn), they're out!

4. The aim is for the raider to make it out again without being wrestled to the ground – anyone who doesn't make it gives a point to the opposite side.

The team with the most points at the end wins!

2. Flip your stick over to tap the ball with the other side while you run. This protects the ball from being hit by anyone else.

3. Repeat until you score!

Amazing South Asians

South Asia and Britain share a long history, with countries such as India, Bangladesh and Pakistan shaping British culture for as long as there has been trade and travel across the globe. Many amazing South Asians have gone on to call Britain home. Here are just a few who have made their mark on history.

ABDUL KARIM
Munsi (teacher) and Advisor to Queen Victoria, 1863–1909

Abdul was one of two Indian servants sent to Britain to serve Queen Victoria in 1887. Over his years of service, Victoria and Abdul became close friends, with Abdul teaching the queen Hindustani, accompanying her on official trips and becoming one of her most important advisors. Members of the royal family tried to drive them apart, but Queen Victoria always supported Abdul. After her death, Victoria's son, King Edward VII, sent Abdul back to India and tried to erase his record from history by having documents, letters and photographs of Abdul destroyed.

PRINCESS SOPHIA DULEEP SINGH
Suffragette, 1876–1948

With a former king of the Sikh Empire as her father, and Queen Victoria as her godmother, Princess Sophia had friends in high places. Although she lived a comfortable life in royal palaces, she was unhappy that British women were not being given the same rights and freedoms as men. She used her place in society to protest against laws she did not think were fair, especially in campaigning for women to have the right to vote.

CORNELIA SORABJI
Lawyer, 1866–1954

Not only was Cornelia the first woman to graduate from the University of Bombay (now known as the University of Mumbai), she was also the first Indian person and first woman to study law at Oxford University. She went on to become the first woman to practise law in India and campaigned in support of education for girls, ending child marriage and for protection of women whose husbands had died.

JAYABEN DESAI

Protester, 1933–2010

While working in a factory in London, Jayaben realised that she was earning less than the white people who were doing the same job. Despite the risk of being fired, she walked out of the factory in protest and urged other people in the same position to join her. She inspired others to be brave and speak up about unfair treatment, and although there are still improvements to be made, Jayaben's protest has led to fairer working conditions for many people.

FREDDIE MERCURY

Musician, 1946–1991

Born to Parsee Indian parents in Stone Town, in Zanzibar, Farrokh Bulsara (as he was then known) moved to West London aged 17 with a passion for music and a talent for piano. He went on to become the lead singer of one of the most iconic rock bands ever known, Queen. Going by the name of Freddie Mercury, he wrote many of their most popular songs. If you've never heard any Queen songs, ask the nearest adult to you to give you a rendition, you won't be disappointed (unless they're really bad at singing)!

ANISH KAPOOR

Sculptor, b. 1954

Born in Bombay (now known as Mumbai) in India, Anish came to England to study when he was a teenager. His sculptures play with ideas of shape and space, and his work has been so influential that he has won the one of the British art world's most important awards, the Turner Prize. Queen Elizabeth II made him a 'knight bachelor' for his service to visual arts in the United Kingdom in 2013.

TALVIN SINGH

Composer and Music Producer, b. 1970

Using traditional Indian instruments like the *tabla* (a type of drum), Talvin makes music that is a mixture of sounds from India and EDM (electronic dance music) from Europe. His unique sound led to him winning one of the most important awards in the British music industry, the Mercury Prize and his career has spanned for decades.

Amazing South Asians Today

Brilliant Indian, Pakistani, Bangladeshi and other people of
South Asian heritage continue to shape Britain, and the world, today.
Some faces you might recognise, but some might be new to you!

SHAMIL AND KAVI THAKRAR
Entrepeneurs, b. 1971 and 1982

Food lovers Shamil and Kavi had noticed that many Indian restaurants in the United Kingdom were serving up similar dishes over and over again. They felt that Indian food and culture had much more to offer, and so with their friends Amar and Adarsh Radia, they started an Indian restaurant like no other. Inspired by the Iranian cafés found in Bombay (now known as Mumbai), in which people from all walks of life rub shoulders and eat together, they opened the first branch of *Dishoom* in 2010, serving delicious Indian 'street food' that many British people had never tried. They have gone on to open many more award-winning restaurants, and since Ramadan in 2015 have donated over 10 million meals to hungry children in both the United Kingdom and India.

RIZ AHMED
Actor and Musician, b. 1982

Born and raised in London, Rizwan worked hard at school and gained a place at one of Britain's top universities to study philosophy, politics and economics. He also developed a love for acting and rap music, which led to his career as a musician (as Riz MC) and an actor, becoming the first Muslim to be nominated for Best Leading Actor at the Oscars. As well as campaigning in support of refugees, he also stands up for the right for Muslim people to be treated fairly and to have the same recognition and creative opportunities as people from other backgrounds.

NADIYA HUSSAIN
Author and Baker, b. 1984

The first ever South Asian winner of the popular TV baking competition, *The Great British Bake Off*, Nadiya has gone on to write many cookbooks for both adults and children (many of them about cakes!) and to host her own TV shows about everything from food pioneers to coping with anxiety. She was born in Luton to a Bangladeshi family and loves mixing flavours together from all different kinds of cultures.

ASH SARKAR
Journalist, Lecturer and Poet, b. 1992

As a journalist and a lecturer, Ash uses her voice to stand up for the things she believes in, such as equal rights for people of all ethnicities. She comes from a family of campaigners, her great-great-aunt was an important figure in the campaign for Indian Independence from British rule.

MALALA YOUSAFZAI
Activist, b. 1997

In the area where Malala grew up in Pakistan, education for girls was not encouraged. A dangerous organisation known as the Taliban would attack schools that taught girls, and anyone involved in running them. Despite this, from the age of 11, with the help of her teacher father, Malala had been writing a secret blog about the importance of going to school. One day, when she was just 15, the Taliban attacked Malala's school bus, and Malala was shot. Immediately after the attack, she was flown to the United Kingdom for life-saving treatment. Surviving made her even more determined to make a difference and ever since her recovery she has campaigned for every girl's right to an education. Malala is the youngest person ever to have received a Nobel Peace Prize.

Positions of Power

In 1892, Dadabhai Naoroji was the first elected South Asian member of British parliament, and in 2022 Rishi Sunak became the United Kingdom's first ever Prime Minister of South Asian heritage. Today, the United Kingdom is governed by more people of South Asian heritage than ever before. Some have worked as government ministers such as Sajid Javid and Priti Patel as Chancellor of the Exchequer and the Home Secretary. In 2016, Sir Sadiq Khan was elected as the first Muslim Mayor of London.

Baroness Shami Chakrabarti, Sir Rabinder Singh and Rishi Sunak.

Among other notable people working hard to uphold the law are Baroness Shami Chakrabarti, a member of the House of Lords, barrister and human rights activist, Sir Rabinder Singh, the first person of colour to be appointed as a judge to the Court of Appeal, and Neil Basu, who has worked as the assistant commissioner for the Metropolitan Police.

A South Asian Calendar of Celebrations

You've probably heard of a solar (or seasonal) year, which is the amount of time that it takes the Earth to travel once around the sun: 12 months, or 365 ¼ days. But have you heard of a lunar year?

A lunar year is counted as 12 complete cycles of the phases of the moon. During one solar year, there are roughly 12.3 cycles of the phases of the moon, which means that the date of any important celebration or event worked out using the lunar calendar will change every solar (or seasonal) year. This method is still used to work out when many important South Asian celebrations and religious festivals are held.

A Few Festivals and Celebrations to Discover

HOLI
March
Also known as the 'festival of love' and a celebration of good over evil, Holi marks the start of spring. The first day involves a special Hindu ceremony around a bonfire, and the second day involves throwing water and brightly coloured power called *gulal* over other people.

BASANTA UTSAV
March
In Bangladesh, the start of spring is celebrated with dance, music and by covering each other's hands and faces with brightly coloured powder.

VIKRAM SAMVAT
Between March and April
The New Year for Hindus.

VAISAKHI
13th or 14th April
The celebration of the year Sikhism was founded (1699) and the Punjabi New Year. Look out for special parades and decorations!

INDEPENDENCE DAY FOR PAKISTAN AND INDIA
14th and 15th August
On 15th August in 1947, India became free from British rule and the country of Pakistan was created. Independence Day is now celebrated in Pakistan on 14th August and India on 15th August.

ONAM
Between August and September
During this Keralan harvest festival, people decorate the ground in front of their homes with flowers and celebrate with feasts and games.

RAKSHA BANDHAN
22nd August

This Hindu festival, also known as *Rakhi*, celebrates the bond between siblings. Traditionally, sisters give their brothers a bracelet called a *rakhi*, and they receive a gift in return. Of course, not everyone has a brother, so it's also common for cousins to share *rakhi* and presents too.

HIJRI (ISLAMIC) NEW YEAR
Changes yearly

Also known as *Muharram*, after the first month of the Islamic calendar, or Arabic New Year. For some Muslims the new year begins when they spot a crescent moon in the sky, but others rely on dates provided by scientists who calculate the moon's movement.

DIWALI
Between October and November

This five-day festival of light is celebrated by Hindus, Jains and Sikhs. People often light special lamps called diyas and set off fireworks.

RAMADAN
Changes yearly

During the ninth month of the Islamic calendar, many adult Muslims don't eat or drink during daylight hours, which is known as fasting. People fast to help them to think about people less fortunate than themselves, and to focus their thoughts on prayer. It can be tough, but it makes family mealtimes once the sun goes down extra special.

EID AL-FITR
Changes yearly

To celebrate the last day of Ramadan after a month of fasting, Muslim families get together for a special time of prayer at a mosque, then share lots of delicious food!

EID AL-ADHA
Changes yearly

This Islamic festival marks the end of the *Hajj* pilgrimage to the holy city of Mecca.

Time to Reflect

Like many countries, the United Kingdom is home to millions of people whose families have, at some point in history, come from all over the world. This brilliant mix of people and cultures affects everything about British life, from the words we use to the food we eat.

A Shared History

It is impossible to separate the history of countries that were invaded and run by the British from British history. Indian history is British history, as is Pakistani history and Bangladeshi history.

The fact that people with links to India, Pakistan, Bangladesh and other countries from around the world play such an important role in British society today is because we are bound together by these shared experiences.

Under British rule, the history of India, Pakistan and Bangladesh wasn't always happy or fair, and at times it was unspeakably terrible. There is so much more to uncover than we could ever have managed to fit into this book, and many stories remain untold.

But our hope is that by starting to understand India, Pakistan, Bangladesh and Britain's complicated history, we can learn how to build a better future, where everyone is valued and treated as being equally important. Being born into a specific culture or part of society doesn't mean we cannot respect or equally be part of another.

Let's Celebrate!

Embracing new people, ideas and customs has made the United Kingdom the place it is today, and that's something to celebrate. Now you know lots of brilliant South Asian-inspired ways how!

YOU COULD...
- Get some friends together for a garba
- Play Kabaddi
- Do some bhangra
- Wear something special
- Go and look for the moon with your family
- Eat some sweets
- Decorate your house with twinkling lights
- Throw some colourful paint

What Happened When?

During ancient Indian history, many empires ruled different parts of modern-day India, Pakistan and Bangladesh, plus some of the surrounding countries. When we talk about ancient India here, we are talking about any land that was ever part of an Indian empire.

By this time, the Harappan people are growing cotton plants and weaving cotton fabric.
(Page 10)

Around 2500 BCE

A very early form of Ayurvedic medicine, in which you care for the body and soul together, starts to be used in ancient India.
(Page 11)

Around 1000 BCE

Trade in cotton begins between the people of ancient India and the ancient Greeks and Romans.
(Page 10)

Around 320s BCE

Around 2700 BCE

Some historians believe an ancient type of yoga starts to be practised by the Harappan people (also known as the Indus Valley Civilization) in the northern part of ancient India.
(Page 34-35)

Around 600 BCE

Evidence shows that advanced surgery, including reconstructing a person's nose, is practised in India at this time.
(Page 11)

Around 320–185 BCE

Rule of the Mauryan Empire, the first empire to cover much of modern India, Pakistan and Bangladesh, as well as some parts of Iran.
(Page 14)

ANCIENT INDIAN EMPIRES

Ancient India was a land made up of many different kingdoms and empires. There were too many for us to have mentioned them all in this book, so we have included just a few key examples.

Rule of the Hindu Gupta Empire, during which many mathematical and scientific discoveries were made, also known as the Golden Age of India.
(Page 11 and 15)

Around 320–550 CE

Rule of the Delhi Sultanate, an Islamic kingdom that built many great cities including one of the tallest minarets in Asia, the Qutb Minar.
(Page 15)

1206–1556

The Mughal Empire takes over parts of India and its rulers try to create a kingdom where people of different faiths live side by side.
(Page 15)

1526–1858

English King Henry VIII decides to rule over Wales as well as England. By 1543, England and Wales are unified.
(Page 7)

1536

Around 30–375 CE

Rule of the Kushan Empire, which spread Buddhism across ancient India.
(Page 14)

Around 400 CE

The seven-metre-tall iron pillar of Delhi is forged.
(Page 10)

628 CE

Brahmagupta, an Indian astronomer, is the first person to define zero as the result of subtracting a number from itself.
(Page 11)

1558–1603

Often called the Elizabethan Age, during which Queen Elizabeth I ruled over England.
(Page 16)

What Happened Next?

By the 1500s, India had been trading goods with other countries for centuries. People had also travelled from India to settle in countries across the world. Records show people of South Asian heritage living in Britain from the middle of the 16th century, however it's very possible that many South Asians lived unrecorded lives in Britain long before this time.

1600 — Queen Elizabeth I gives 218 British merchants permission to form a business known as the East India Company. (Page 16)

1601 — The East India Company's first five trading ships depart Britain for the Spice Islands, known today as *Malaku* or the Moluccas. (Page 16)

1608 — The East India Company's first ships arrive in Surat, India. (Page 16)

1674–1818 — A Hindu warrior group called the Maratha go on to build an empire which covers much of central and northern India. (Page 15)

1707 — Scotland is unified with England and Wales and the three counties become Great Britain. (Page 7)

1730s–1770s — The East India Company transports enslaved people from Africa (as well as Indonesia) to other countries where they are forced to work for no pay. (Page 17)

1765 — The Treaty of Allahabad is signed giving the East India Company the right to collect taxes from the people of Bengal (West Bengal and Bangladesh), Bihar and Orissa (now known as Odisha). (Page 18)

1799–1849 — Located in what would be modern-day Pakistan, the Sikh Empire was founded by Ranjit Singh, one-time owner of the world-famous *Koh-i-Noor* diamond. (Page 15)

1801 — Ireland is unified with Great Britain (Wales, Scotland and England) and the four countries become known as the United Kingdom. (Page 7)

1807

The slave trade is made illegal in the United Kingdom, meaning no British ships or British subjects can trade in enslaved people. Slavery continues in the British colonies.
(Page 17)

1833

Slavery is finally abolished in the British colonies.
(Page 17)

1858

The British government takes control of India from the East India Company. India becomes part of the British Empire.
(Page 20)

1910

Princess Sophia Duleep Singh marches to Parliament Square in London, England, with more than 300 suffragettes as part of the campaign for women's right to vote.
(Page 50)

1920–1922

Ireland is partitioned by the British government into Northern Ireland, which remains part of the United Kingdom, and Southern Ireland (known today as the Republic of Ireland or Éire).
(Page 7)

1837–1901

Queen Victoria rules over the United Kingdom.
(Page 19)

1857

After many failed attempts to fight for freedom, the Indian War of Independence against British rule under the East India Company forces the British government to step in.
(Page 19)

1892

Dadabhai Naoroji becomes the first Indian member of parliament in Britain.
(Page 53)

1914–1918

The First World War begins, and soldiers from across the British Empire, including India, come to Britain's aid.
(Pages 22–23)

The Colour Bar is lifted in the United Kingdom.
(Page 32)

East Pakistan becomes an independent country and changes its name to Bangladesh.
(Page 27)

Sir Sadiq Khan, the first Muslim Mayor of London.

India becomes independent of British rule and at the same time is partitioned by the British government, creating the country of Pakistan. Around 15 million people are forced to leave their homes.
(Pages 24–27)

Jawaharlal Nehru becomes the first prime minister of India.

In 2016, the people of London, England, elected their first ever Mayor of South Asian heritage, Sadiq Khan. He was knighted in 2025. In 2022, the first Prime Minister of South Asian heritage, Rishi Sunak, took charge of the British government.
(Page 53)

1947   **1966**   **1971**   **Now**

1939–1945

The Second World War plunges the world into turmoil for a second time. Once again, soldiers from across the British Empire, including India, come to Britain's aid.
(Pages 22–23)

1948

Campaigner for an independent and united India, Mahatma Gandhi is shot dead in Delhi by a stranger who disagreed with his beliefs.
(Page 24)

1962

The Commonwealth Immigration Act becomes law in the United Kingdom. This was the first of many laws passed in the 1960s that made it harder and harder for people from the Commonwealth to make Britain their home.
(Pages 30)

1979

A group fighting against racism in Southall, London, in England, stand up to the police and the National Front.
(Pages 32–33)

Glossary

archaeologist Someone who studies history by examining objects of the past, which they have often dug up from the ground.

ayah A South Asian nanny employed by wealthy European families.

Ayurvedic medicine An ancient Indian approach to healthcare where the body and soul are looked after together.

borders Invisible lines that separate one country from another.

British Raj The rule of the British royal family over India (now known as India, Pakistan and Bangladesh) between 1858 and 1947. During this time, the people of India were forced to live under laws made by the British government.

climate Types of weather patterns, for example warm or wet, generally associated with a country or region.

Colour Bar Informal rules made by businesses and organisations that meant in cities across Great Britain there were places that people of colour were not allowed to work or visit.

conquer To overcome a country or piece of land by force.

continent One of the world's seven geographical regions. They consist of Asia, Africa, North and South America, Europe, Antarctica and Oceania.

decimal system Also called the Hindu-Arabic numeral system, this way of writing figures uses the numbers 0, 1, 2, 3, 4, 5, 6, 7, 8 and 9, and came to replace Roman numerals.

East India Company Founded in 1600 by the British to trade with southeast Asia and India

empire A group of countries or regions that are ruled by the royal family or government of a single country.

First World War The first global war lasting between 1914–1918 was fought between the Central Powers (Germany, Austro-Hungary and Turkey) and the Allies (France, Great Britain, Russia, Italy and Japan, and from 1917 the United States of America).

identity Things that make someone a unique individual, including their appearance, personality and beliefs.

Indian subcontinent The part of the world now made up of the countries India, Pakistan and Bangladesh.

kingdom A country, state or territory with a ruling body led by a king or queen.

lascar A South Asian sailor employed on the sea voyages between the Indian subcontinent and Great Britain.

nomad A person with no fixed home, who travels from place to place to find food for themselves and their animals.

Partition Splitting a country into parts.

racism Treating a person differently because of the colour of their skin, the country they come from, or the ethnic group to which they belong.

refugee A person who has been forced to leave their country for their own safety due to their race, religion or ethnicity, to escape a war, or as the result of a natural disaster.

Roman numerals A way of writing numbers, with letters representing numbers instead. I = 1, V = 5 and X = 10, and so on.

Second World War The second global war lasting between 1939–1945 was fought between the Axis Powers (Germany, Italy and Japan) and the Allied Powers (France, Great Britain, the United States and Russia).

segregation The separation of one group of people from another due to race, class or ethnicity.

Silk Roads An important ancient trade route that passed through the Indian subcontinent, connecting China to the east and Arabian ports to the west.

slavery The transportation and trade of enslaved people from their homes in Africa, Indonesia and other countries, to new countries where they were forced to work for no money and were treated extremely badly.

spices Vegetable products including leaves, seeds, roots, fruit or bark with a strong taste and smell used to flavour food, such as black pepper, chilli, cinnamon or ginger. Spices are often dried and ground.

state Part of a country that has its own land and government, which enables the people living there to make their own laws and to follow their own religion.

treaty A formal agreement between countries or states about who will be in charge, usually made at the end of a long-term disagreement or war.

Index

A
Alexander the Great 10
Ancient Greek 10, 11, 58
army 17, 18, 20, 24
    British 22, 23, 48
Ayurvedic medicine 11, 58, 63

B
Bandi Chhor Divas 40
battle 18, 23
border 6, 26, 63
Brahmagupta 11, 59
Brahman 12
British government 17, 19, 20, 23, 24, 25, 30, 33, 53, 61, 62, 63
British rule 20, 21, 22, 24, 53, 54, 57, 61, 62

C
celebration 31, 39, 40–41, 45, 54–55
Commonwealth 21, 30, 62
communities 25, 30, 31, 32, 34
cotton 10, 16, 21, 43, 58
culture 33, 34, 42–43, 44, 50, 52, 56
customs 33, 44–45, 57

D
dance 29, 35, 38–39, 40, 51, 54
decimal system 11, 15, 59, 63
Diwali 31, 40, 55

E
East India Company 16–17, 18–19, 20, 28, 42, 43, 60, 61, 63
Eid al-Fitr 41, 45, 55
emperor 14, 15, 18, 20, 48
empire 14–15, 20–21, 63
    British 21, 22, 24, 26, 27, 48, 61, 62
    Mauryan Empire 14, 58
    Kushan Empire 14, 59
    Gupta Empire 15, 59
    Mughal Empire 15, 59
    Maratha Empire 15, 58
    Sikh Empire 15, 50, 60

F
fasting 13, 40, 41, 55
First World War 22–23, 61, 63
food 19, 26, 28, 30, 31, 34, 36–37, 40–41, 43, 52, 54, 55, 56, 57, 63
freedom 20, 22, 24, 40, 50, 61

G
games 9, 11, 43, 48–49, 54, 57
Gandhi, Mahatma 24, 62
Golden Age of India 15, 59

H
Harappan people 10, 58
Hijri 55
Hippocrates 11
Holi 54

I
immigrants 28–29, 32, 33, 34
independence 22, 24, 25, 26–27, 53, 54
Indian War of Independence 19, 20, 61
invention 10, 11

J
Jinnah, Muhammad Ali 24

K
karma 12, 13
Koh-i-Noor diamond 15, 60

L
language 9, 14, 32, 33, 46–47
laws 14, 19, 24, 30, 32, 50, 62

M
massage 35, 42
merchants 16, 28, 29, 60
mosque 6, 31, 55
music 34, 38–39, 40, 51, 52, 54

N
Naoroji, Dadabhai 53, 61

P
Partition 24–25, 26–27, 30, 36, 61, 62, 63
pilgrimage 13, 55

Q
queen 14, 15, 17
    Elizabeth I 16, 59, 60
    Victoria 19, 20, 29, 31, 43, 50, 61
    Elizabeth II 51

R
racism 32–33, 63
Radcliffe, Cyril 25
Ramadan 13, 41, 52, 55
reincarnation 12, 13
religion 8, 9, 12–13, 14, 24, 25, 26, 40–41, 45
    Buddhism 12, 14, 41, 59
    Christianity 12, 13, 28
    Hinduism 9, 12, 14, 15, 24, 25, 40, 54, 55, 59
    Islam 12, 13, 15, 24, 25, 41, 55, 59
    Jainism 12, 40
    Sikhism 12, 13, 15, 24, 25, 40, 41, 54
religious festivals 40–41, 54–55

S
Second World War 22, 23, 24, 31, 43, 62, 63
segregation 32, 62, 63
ships 16, 17, 28, 29, 30, 31, 60, 61
Silk Roads 14, 63
slavery 17, 20, 60, 61, 63
spices 6, 10, 16, 17, 20, 21, 35, 36, 37, 60, 63

T
taxes 18, 19, 60
temple 6, 31, 41

V
Vaisakhi 41, 56
Vesak 41
Vikram Samvat 56

Y
yoga 6, 34–35, 47, 58

A NOTE FROM THE AUTHORS

It would be impossible to cover the whole of Indian, Pakistani, Bangladeshi and British history in just one book. We have done our best to touch on and explain key moments in the complex history of these four countries, which we hope will inspire readers of all ages to find out more. While every care has been taken to ensure the accuracy of content at the time of going to press, as we learn more about history and revaluate our findings, some information may change. In other cases there is so much conflicting information that it may never be possible to make an entirely accurate statement.
Like all good investigators, we are open to new research that may change how we understand the past.